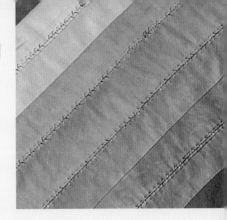

Contents

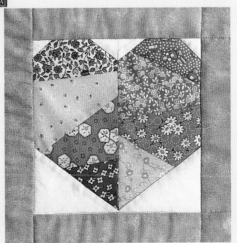

Sail Off to Sleep

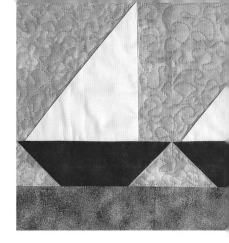

Paper-pieced block quilt

*L*iving on a lake in northern Minnesota, I spend much of my free time relaxing on the shore and watching the water. On breezy mornings, the sailboats often venture out to take advantage of nature's power and glide quietly across the waves. Small children, particularly little boys, love boats, so it seemed like a fitting subject for a baby quilt. The sailboat, with its geometric lines, was easy to design as a foundation-pieced pattern. The blocks can be sewn together quickly. You can follow my color scheme or choose several colors for the boat bodies.

Sharon Hultgren

FINISHED SIZE: 40" × 49" (102 × 125 cm)

TECHNIQUES USED: Foundation piecing, stipple quilting or method of choice, mitered-corner binding

Cutting Directions

Light blue sky fabric; cut into smaller pieces at least 1/2" (1.3 cm) larger than each of the four sky areas in the block (16 of each piece)

Eight 9" (23 cm) squares of white fabric, cut in half diagonally

Sixteen 3" × 8" (7.5 × 20.5 cm) rectangles of red fabric

Three 2 1/2" (6.5 cm) full crosswise strips of medium blue for water

Four 2" (5 cm) full crosswise strips of yellow fabric for inner borders

Four 1 1/2" (3.8 cm) full crosswise strips of red fabric for middle borders

Four 3 1/2" (9 cm) full crosswise strips of medium blue fabric for outer borders

Four or five 2 1/2" (6.5 cm) full crosswise strips of medium blue fabric for binding

Materials

- Foundation-piecing paper
- 1/2 yd. (0.5 m) white fabric for sails
- 2/3 yd. (0.63 m) red fabric for boats and middle borders
- 1 yd. (0.92 m) light blue fabric for sky
- 1/3 yd. (0.32 m) yellow fabric for inner border
- 1 yd. (0.92 m) medium blue fabric for water, outer border, and binding
- 1 1/4 yd. (1.15 m) fabric for backing
- One low-loft crib batting

1. Trace or copy the pattern (page 7) onto foundation-piecing paper. Trace the pattern eight times; trace the mirror image of the pattern eight times.

2. Place a piece of blue sky fabric, right side up, on the blank side of the pattern, over area #1; pin. Fold the fabric and pattern on the sewing line between #1 and #2. This will help you set the second piece in place.

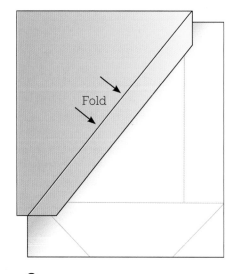

Fold

2

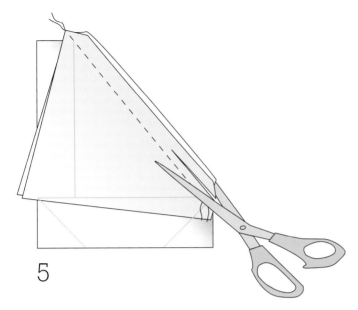

5

3. Place a white triangle over the blue, right sides together; pin along the sewing line. Flip the white fabric over to be sure it will cover area #2; adjust if necessary. Flip the white fabric back in place.

4. From the printed side of the pattern, stitch on the line between areas #1 and #2. Use a short stitch length and stitch a few stitches beyond the ends of the line.

5. With the block printed side up, turn the pattern back on the stitching line and trim the seam allowances to ¼" (6 mm).

6. Fold the pattern back in place. Turn the white fabric over area #2; pin.

7. Apply the fabric for area #3, following steps 3 to 6. Continue until all the areas have been applied.

8. Press the block. Trim away the excess fabric, leaving a ¼" (6 mm) seam allowance beyond the outer pattern line. Carefully tear away the paper pattern.

9. Repeat steps 2 to 8 for all the boat blocks. Sew the boats into four rows of four boats each, with boats in each row facing the same direction. Press the seam allowances open.

10. Measure the rows. Cut all the water strips the same length as the shortest row. Sew the boats and water strips together, alternating the direction of the boats with each row. Match the ends of the strips to the ends of the rows and ease in any excess length. Make sure the blocks align vertically.

11. Measure the quilt top to bottom through the center. Cut two yellow strips to this length. Sew these inner border pieces to the sides of the quilt. Press the seam allowances toward the border.

Designer's Tip

There are several special papers made for foundation piecing. There is even paper that can be dissolved in water after the quilt is sewn! If you use a copy machine to copy the pattern from the book, check the pattern to be sure it has not changed in size. If you copy the pattern by hand, use a pencil, never a ballpoint pen, as the ink can transfer to your fabric.

12. Measure the quilt side to side through the center, including the side inner borders. Cut two yellow strips to this length. Sew the inner border pieces to the top and bottom of the quilt. Press the seam allowances toward the border.

13. Attach the red middle border, following the procedure in steps 11 and 12. Repeat for the outer blue border.

14. Press the quilt. Cut batting and backing slightly larger than the quilt top. Layer the backing, batting, and quilt top; baste with safety pins or by hand. Quilt by machine, outlining the blocks and borders and stipple-quilting the sky. Or use your quilting method of choice.

15. Join the binding strips with ¼" (6 mm) diagonal seams to minimize bulk; press the seam allowances open. Press the binding in half lengthwise, wrong sides together.

16. Stitch the binding to the quilt front, stitching ⅜" (1 cm) from the edge; begin on one side about 3" (7.5 cm) from the end of the binding. At each corner, stop stitching at the exact center of the corner; backstitch two stitches. Fold the binding back diagonally, and then fold it down along the next edge. Start stitching again at the center of the corner, and continue.

17. Stop about 3" (7.5 cm) from the starting point. Mark dots on the inside of the binding fold where the beginning and end would meet. Unfold the binding. Place the beginning and end right sides together, perpendicular to each other, aligning the dots. Stitch diagonally across the strips. Trim the seam allowances to ¼" (6 mm) and press open. Refold the binding and finish stitching it in place.

18. Wrap the binding to the back of the quilt, just covering the stitching line with the binding fold and mitering the corners. Stitch in the ditch from the right side.

17

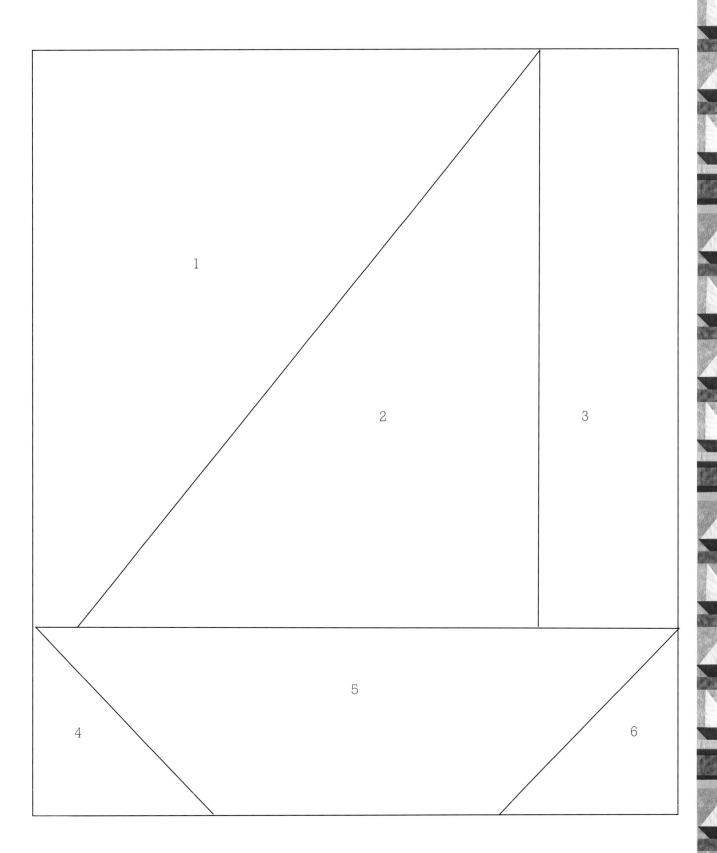

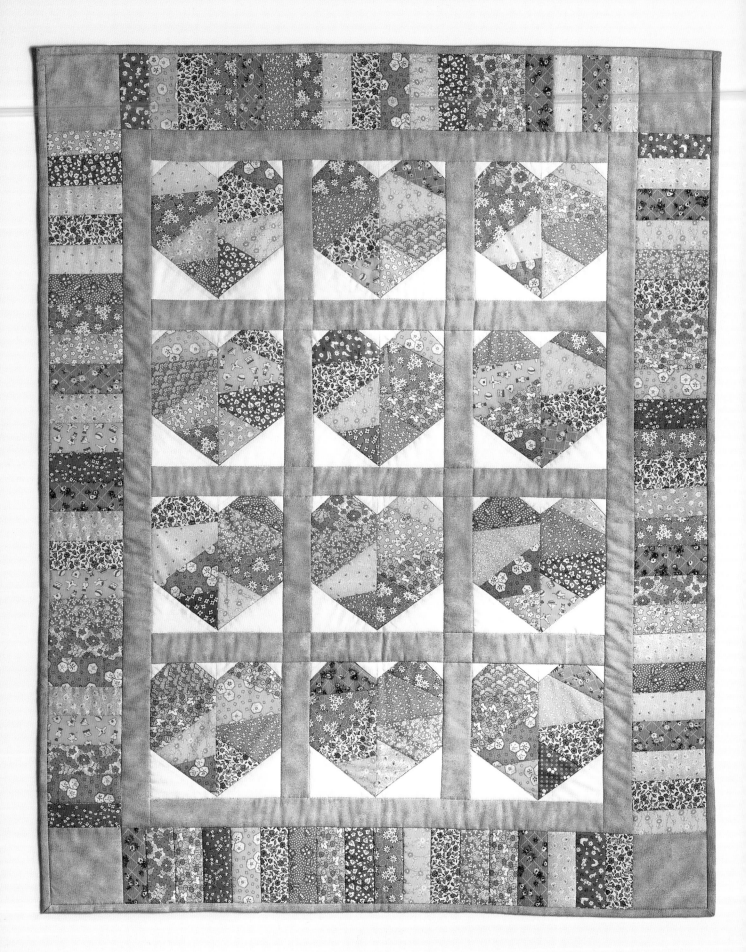

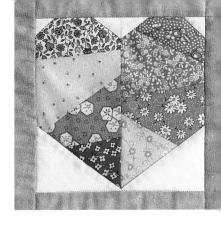

Little Sweetheart

Paper-pieced block quilt

etro-print pastel fabrics
are so sweet and sentimental. I just can't get
enough of them, so I was able to pull quite
a few from my stash to use in this quilt (I think there
are about twenty!). If you don't have a stash like mine
to pull from, buy a minimum of eight different fabrics
in assorted colors for the pieced hearts. By alternating
the fabrics for each area and shuffling them around,
you can create twelve unique hearts. The color of the
sashing, inner borders, and corner squares can easily
be changed to blue for a baby boy or to any other color
to match the nursery.

Sharon Hultgren

FINISHED SIZE: 35" × 43½" (89 × 110.3 cm)

TECHNIQUES USED: Foundation piecing, piano key border,
mitered-corner binding

Materials

- Foundation-piecing paper
- Eight to 12 fat quarters 18" × 22" (46 × 56 cm) of assorted pastel retro-print fabrics
- ½ yd. (0.5 m) cream fabric for background
- 1 yd. (0.92 m) fabric for sashing, inner border, and binding
- 1½ yd. (1.4 m) fabric for backing
- One low-loft crib batting

Cutting Directions

12 pastel print pieces at least ½" (1.3 cm) larger than each of the eight heart areas in the blocks; alternate fabrics so the same print is not repeated in each heart

Twelve 5" (12.7 cm) squares of cream background fabric; cut in half diagonally

Twenty-four 2½" (6.5 cm) squares of cream background fabric; cut in half diagonally

Nine 2" (5 cm) full crosswise strips of sashing/inner border fabric; cut two of the strips into eight 7½" (19.3 cm) pieces

Eighty-eight 2" × 4½" (5 × 11.5 cm) assorted pastel print rectangles for piano key border

Four 4½" (11.5 cm) squares of sashing/inner border fabric

Four 2½" (6.5 cm) full crosswise strips of binding fabric

1. Trace or copy the patterns (page 12) onto foundation-piecing paper. You will need twelve of each pattern.

2. Arrange the pieces for each heart half in the order in which they will be sewn.

3. Place the fabric piece for area #1, right side up, on the blank side of the pattern, over area #1; pin. Fold the fabric and pattern on the sewing line between #1 and #2. This will help you set the second piece in place.

4. Place the fabric piece for area #2 over the first fabric, right sides together; pin along the sewing line. Flip the second fabric over to be sure it will cover area #2; adjust if necessary. Flip the second fabric back in place.

5. From the printed side of the pattern, stitch on the line between areas #1 and #2. Use a short stitch length and stitch a few stitches beyond the ends of the line.

6. With the block printed side up, turn the pattern back on the stitching line and trim the seam allowances to ¼" (6 mm).

7. Fold the pattern back in place. Turn the second fabric over area #2; pin.

8. Apply the fabric for area #3, following steps 4 to 7. Continue until all the areas have been applied.

9. Press the block. Trim away the excess fabric, leaving a ¼" (6 mm) seam allowance beyond the outer pattern line.

10. Repeat steps 3 to 9 for all the heart halves. Then sew the halves together to make 12 hearts. Carefully tear away the paper pattern. Press the center seam allowances apart.

11. Arrange the hearts in four rows of three hearts each. Join the hearts in each row by stitching a short sashing strip between them. Press the seam allowances toward the sashing strips.

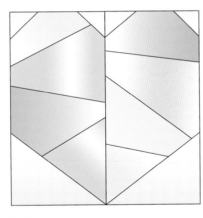

10

Designer's Tip

Tear away the paper one area at a time, working from the last area sewn to the first. Crease the paper along each seam and then gently tear along the sewn, perforated edge.

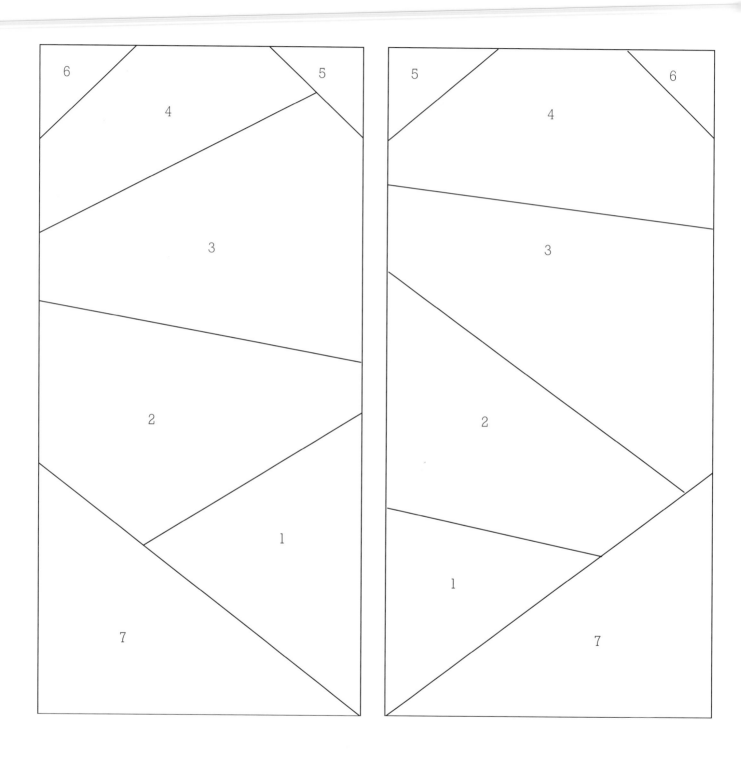

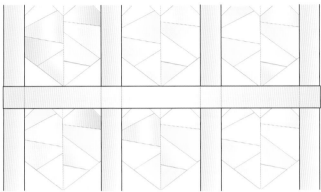

12

12. Measure the width of the heart rows. Cut five of the long sashing strips to the measurement of the shortest row. Join the rows by stitching sashing strips between the rows; add a sashing strip to the top and bottom. Match the ends of the strips to the ends of the rows and ease in any excess length. Make sure the blocks align vertically.

13. Measure the quilt top to bottom through the center. Cut two inner border strips to this length. Sew the inner borders to the sides of the quilt. Press the seam allowances toward the border.

14. Sew the "piano keys" together, using ¼" (6 mm) seams and alternating fabrics. You will need 24 keys for each side border and 18 keys for the top and bottom borders. Check to see that the borders fit; trim the last keys slightly if necessary.

15. Mark the centers of the quilt sides. Mark the centers of the side borders. Pin the borders to the sides, matching centers and ends. Stitch in place; press the seam allowances toward the inner border.

16. Stitch the squares to the ends of the top and bottom borders; press the seam allowances toward the squares. Stitch the top and bottom borders in place, aligning the corners of the squares to the corners of the inner borders. Press the seam allowances toward the inner borders.

17. Press the quilt. Cut batting and backing slightly larger than the quilt top. Layer the backing, batting, and quilt top; baste with safety pins or by hand. Quilt by machine, outlining the blocks and borders.

18. Bind the quilt following steps 15 to 18 on page 6.

Diamonds Bright

String-pieced block quilt

Babies love colors as much as quilters do. This quilt is sure to make any baby happy, boy or girl. The blocks of diagonal stripes are sewn by string piecing on a foundation. The hand-dyed fabrics that I used are slightly muted with a subtle sueded look that invites you to touch them. When the blocks are arranged and sewn together, they create a dynamic diamond design. Decorative stitching with variegated thread creates a little surface texture. The result is a nice mixture of traditional piecing and contemporary use of color. This is a quilt that can grow up with the child and later become a wall hanging or a décor accent.

Sharon Hultgren

FINISHED SIZE: 43" × 43" (109 × 109 cm)

TECHNIQUES USED: String piecing on a foundation, quilting with decorative machine stitches

Materials

- Foundation-piecing paper
- Six fat quarters 18" × 22" (46 × 56 cm) in assorted hand-dyed colors
- ½ yd. (0.5 m) rosy red fabric for first border
- ¾ yd. (0.7 m) bluebird blue fabric for second border and binding
- ½ yd. (0.5 m) medium green fabric for center strip of block and outer border
- ¼ yd. (0.25 m) yellow fabric for narrow accent border
- 1⅓ yd. (1.23 m) fabric for backing
- One low-loft crib batting
- Variegated thread

Cutting Directions

Six 2¼" (6 cm) full-width strips of medium green fabric; cut into three equal pieces for centers of blocks

Ten 1¾" (4.5 cm) crosswise strips from each of the six fat quarters for blocks

Eight 3" (7.5 cm) squares of red; cut in half diagonally to yield 16 triangles

Eight 3" (7.5 cm) squares of blue; cut in half diagonally to yield 16 triangles

Four 1½" (3.8 cm) full crosswise strips of yellow for accent border

Four 3" (7.5 cm) full crosswise strips of red for first border

Four 3" (7.5 cm) full crosswise strips of blue for second border

Four 3" (7.5 cm) full crosswise strips of green for outer border

Four 2½" (6.5 cm) full crosswise strips of blue binding

1. Trace or copy the pattern (page 19) 16 times onto foundation-piecing paper.

2. Place a green fabric strip, right side up, on the blank side of the pattern, over area #1; pin. Fold the fabric and pattern on the sewing line between #1 and #2. This will help you set the second piece in place.

3. Place a fabric strip for area #2 over the first fabric, right sides together; pin along the sewing line. Flip the second fabric over to be sure it will cover area #2; adjust if necessary. Flip the second fabric back in place.

4. From the printed side of the pattern, stitch on the line between areas #1 and #2. Use a short stitch length and stitch a few stitches beyond the ends of the line.

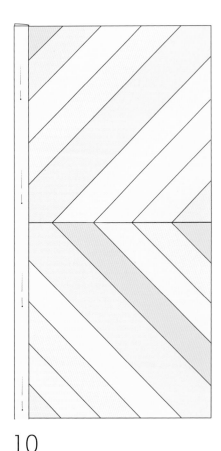

10

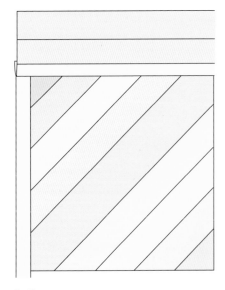

12

5. With the block printed side up, turn the pattern back on the stitching line and trim the seam allowances to ¼" (6 mm).

6. Fold the pattern back in place. Turn the second fabric over area #2; pin.

7. Apply a fabric strip to area #3, following steps 3 to 6. Continue until all the areas have been applied, using one strip of each of the six colors and adding them in random order. Finish the corners with one red and one blue triangle.

8. String-piece all the blocks, adding colors in different arrangements, but always starting with green in the center and ending with red and blue triangles. No two blocks will be the same. Press the blocks. Trim away the excess fabric, leaving a ¼" (6 mm) seam allowance beyond the outer pattern line. Carefully tear away the paper pattern.

9. Arrange the blocks in a pleasing order. The blocks will form a diagonal pattern with alternating red and blue squares at the centers. Sew the blocks together in rows; press the seam allowances open. Then sew the rows together; press the seam allowances open.

10. Measure the pieced quilt; it should be a 28½" (72.3 cm) square. Cut yellow strips to this length. Press the strips in half lengthwise, wrong sides together. Pin them to the sides of the quilt.

11. Sew a red border strip to a blue border strip; press the seam allowances toward the blue. Repeat with the remaining strips to make four sets. Cut the sets to the same length as the yellow strips.

12. Sew a red-blue border set to the top, catching the raw edges of the yellow strip in the seam. Press the seam allowances toward the red. Repeat at the bottom of the quilt. The folded edge of the yellow strip is not stitched down.

13. From the extra pieces of red and blue, cut eight 3" (7.5 cm) sets. Sew these sets into four four-patch squares. Sew the pieced squares to the ends of the remaining pieced borders, alternating colors. Sew these borders to the quilt sides; press the seam allowances toward the borders.

14. Center a green border strip on one side of the quilt. Stitch, beginning and ending ¼" (6 mm) from each corner. Press the seam allowances toward the green. Repeat on each side of the quilt.

15. Fold the quilt top in half diagonally so the border strips overlap at the ends; pin. Mark a line from the point where you stopped stitching to the outer edge of the border. Stitch on the line. Trim the seam allowances to ¼" (6 mm) and press them open. Repeat at each corner to form miters.

16. Cut batting and backing slightly larger than the quilt top. Layer the backing, batting, and quilt top; baste with safety pins or by hand.

17. Thread the top and bobbin of your sewing machine with variegated thread. Quilt by sewing a decorative stitch over the seams of the blocks. Then stitch in the ditch of the border seams.

18. Bind the quilt, following steps 15 to 18 on page 6.

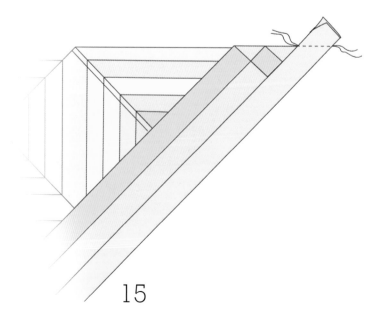

15

Designer's Tip

Decorative machine stitches used for quilting give your project extra color and texture. I used a feather stitch to quilt and stitched on every other line. Even if you have a machine that only has utility stitches, such as stretch stitches, multi-stitch zigzag, blanket stitch, and hemming stitches, some of them may be suitable for quilting. Experiment with the stitches on your machine to see what you like.

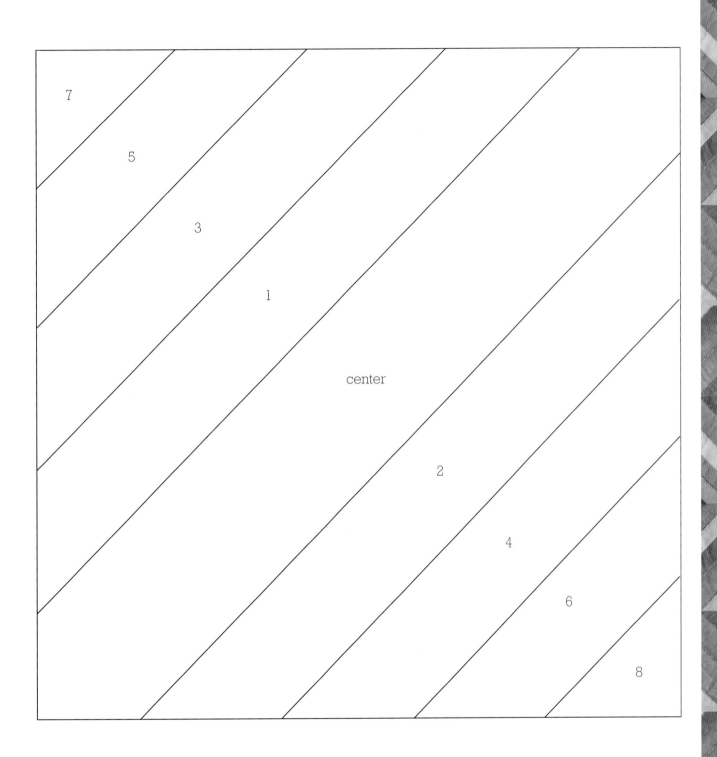

7

5

3

1

center

2

4

6

8

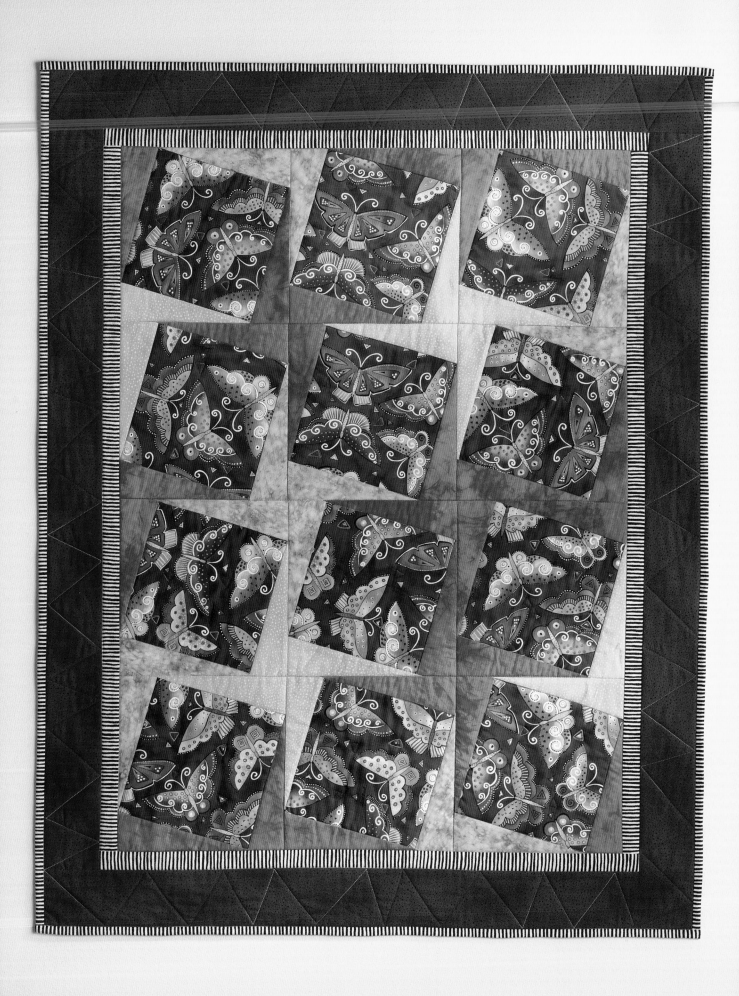

Magic Stars

Contemporary pieced quilt

This lively baby quilt looks complicated but is really easy to make. Choose a brightly patterned fabric for the featured squares and then pick four star fabrics and borders in colors found in the print. The four-pointed stars appear when you put the blocks together. Just lay out the pieces before you sew to keep the colors in order.

Susan Stein

FINISHED SIZE: 35" × 44" (89 × 112 cm)

TECHNIQUES USED: Contemporary piecing, quilting with variegated thread

Materials

- 1 yd. (0.92 m) feature fabric
- ⅓ yd. (0.32 m) each of four fabrics for stars
- ¼ yd. (0.25 m) fabric for inner border
- ½ yd. (0.5 m) fabric for outer border
- ½ yd. (0.5 m) fabric for binding
- 1⅓ yd. (1.23 m) fabric for backing
- See-through template plastic
- Permanent black marker
- Quilter's ruler
- Rotary cutter and cutting mat
- One low-loft crib batting
- Variegated thread

Cutting Directions

Twelve 7¾" (20 cm) squares of feature fabric

Twelve strips 2¾" (7 cm) wide and about 8½" (21.8 cm) long from each star fabric

Four 1½" (3.8 cm) full crosswise strips of inner border fabric

Four 3½" (9 cm) full crosswise strips of outer border fabric

Four 2½" (6.5 cm) full crosswise strips of binding fabric

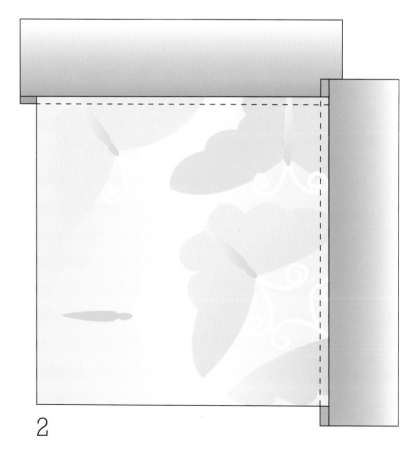

2

1. Sew a strip of star fabric to a feature fabric square. Turn the seam allowances away from the square.

2. Sew a second strip of star fabric (keeping your colors in order) to the second side of the square, extending the strip about ½" (1.3 cm) beyond each edge of the square. At one end, the second strip overlaps the first strip. Turn the seam allowances away from the square.

3. Sew the third and fourth strips to the square in the same way, always keeping the seam allowances turned away from the center square.

4. Repeat steps 1 to 3 for the remaining 11 blocks, keeping your colors in the order you planned. Press the blocks carefully.

5. Make a template for trimming the blocks by drawing a 9½" (24.3 cm) square on the plastic with the marker. Draw a second line ¼" (6 mm) inside of the first line to indicate seam allowances. On the inner line, mark a dot 2" (5 cm) from the left-hand corner on each side. Cut out the square on the outside line.

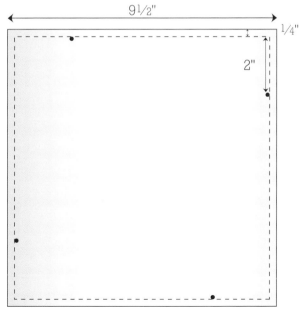

5

6. Lay the template on the block, with the dots at the corners of the center square. Use the marker to draw around the template.

7. Lay the ruler on the lines and use a rotary cutter to trim off the excess fabric around the block. The block should measure 9½" (24.3 cm).

8. Repeat steps 6 and 7 for the remaining 11 blocks.

9. Sew the blocks together into rows. Sew the rows together, aligning the seams. Press the quilt top thoroughly.

10. Measure the quilt top to bottom through the center. Cut two inner border strips to this length. Sew the inner borders to the sides of the quilt. Press the seam allowances toward the borders.

11. Measure the quilt side to side through the center, including the side borders. Cut two inner border strips to this length. Sew the inner borders to the top and bottom of the quilt. Press the seam allowances toward the borders.

12. Attach the outer border, following the procedure in steps 10 and 11.

13. Cut batting and backing slightly larger than the quilt top. Layer the backing, batting, and quilt top; baste with safety pins or by hand.

14. Thread the top and bobbin of your sewing machine with variegated thread. Quilt by stitching in the ditch of all the seams. Quilt random zigzag lines in the outer border and several small triangles in each feature square.

15. Bind the quilt, beginning with the sides and then the top and bottom.

Designer's Tip

Wash or rinse your fabrics in warm water and machine dry. This will prevent shifting of the grain, bleeding of excess dyes, and puckering when the quilt is laundered later. If possible, preshrink the batting also. Press the fabrics thoroughly before cutting to ensure a crisp look and accurate cutting.

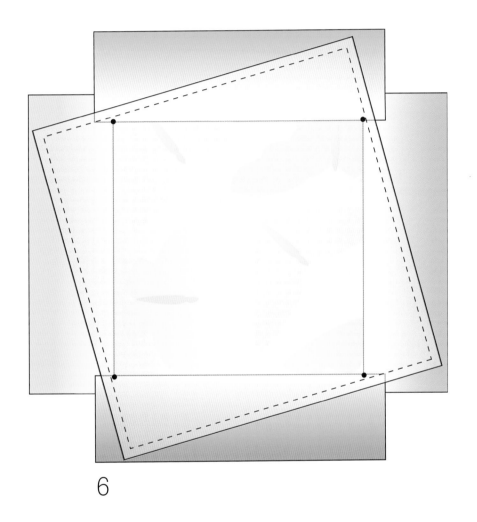

6

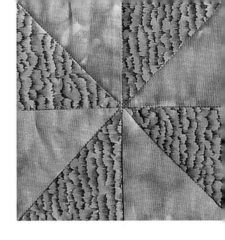

Puzzle Blocks

Triangle squares quilt

*L*ook at all the fun you can have with triangle squares. This project is like a sampler quilt showing six different ways of arranging the same number of triangle squares to create a totally different look in each block. Each block also uses different color combinations, yet they are all tied together with a happy print border.

Susan Stein

FINISHED SIZE: 38" × 52" (96.5 × 132 cm)

TECHNIQUES USED: Grid-pieced triangle squares, quilting with variegated thread

Cutting Directions

Four 9" (23 cm) squares from each of the light and dark fabrics

Seven 2½" (6.5 cm) full crosswise strips of the sashing fabric; from three of the strips, cut nine 12½" (31.8 cm) strips; cut the remaining four strips 30½" (77.3 cm) long

Four 4½" (11.5 cm) full crosswise strips of border fabric

Five 2½" (6.5 cm) full crosswise strips of binding fabric; piece the side binding strips with diagonal seams

Materials

- ¼ yd. (0.25 m) each of three light or warm colored fabrics
- ¼ yd. (0.25 m) each of three darker or cool colored fabrics
- ⅝ yd. (0.6 m) fabric for sashing
- ¾ yd. (0.7 m) fabric for border
- 1⅝ yd. (1.5 m) fabric for backing
- ½ yd. (0.5 m) fabric for binding
- Foundation-piecing paper
- One low-loft crib batting
- Variegated thread

4

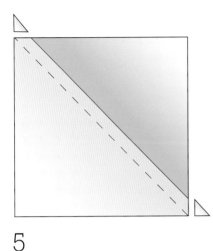

5

Designer's Tip

The seam of the triangle-square is on the bias, so take care when pressing it so it doesn't stretch and ripple. Rather than sliding the iron down the length of the seam, turn the seam allowances to one side and press them in place, moving the iron in the direction of the grain lines.

1. Match up two different squares of block fabric—one light and one dark, or one cool and one warm—for a total of 12 combinations. You will have to repeat some. Place the pairs of fabrics right sides together.

2. Make 12 copies of the stitching guide on page 30. If you draw them by hand, begin with a 7¾" (20 cm) square. If you copy them using a copy machine, make sure the size is not distorted. Pin one sheet of the stitching guide to each pair of block fabrics, using two pins in the center and a pin at each corner.

3. Sew on all of the dashed lines of the stitching guide, using a short stitch length. If your stitch length is too long, it will be difficult to remove the paper after sewing.

4. Cut on all of the solid lines of the stitching guide, through all of the layers. Carefully tear away the paper pattern from the triangles.

5. Press the triangle-squares with the seam allowances to one side. Trim off the "dog ears." Keep the colors sorted into stacks.

6. Create six stacks of two color combinations each. One color should be present in both combinations.

7. Sew the triangle-squares together into blocks arranged in different ways, as shown in the photo on page 26. Press.

8. Arrange the blocks on a design wall or work surface, balancing colors.

9. Sew short sashing strips between each pair of blocks and at the ends of the rows. Press the seam allowances toward the sashing.

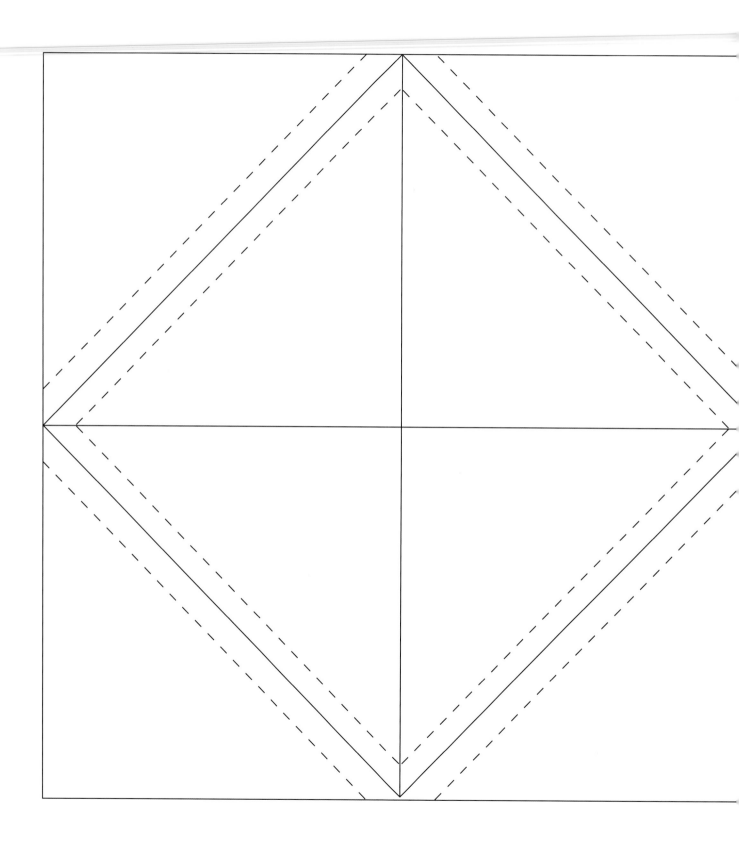

10. Sew the long sashing strips between the rows of blocks and at the top and bottom of the quilt. Make sure the blocks align vertically.

11. Measure the quilt top to bottom through the center. Cut two border strips to this length. Sew the borders to the sides of the quilt. Press the seam allowances toward the borders.

12. Measure the quilt side to side through the center, including the side borders. Cut two border strips to this length. Sew the borders to the top and bottom of the quilt. Press the seam allowances toward the borders.

13. Cut batting and backing slightly larger than the quilt top. Layer the backing, batting, and quilt top; baste with safety pins or by hand.

14. Thread the top and bobbin of your sewing machine with variegated thread. Quilt by stitching in the ditch of all the sashing seams and around each block. Quilt each block in a pattern that suits the arrangement of the triangle-squares. Stitch crisscrossing wavy lines in the border.

15. Bind the quilt, beginning with the sides and then the top and bottom.